# Kim and Kat Get Fit

Written by **Phillip Simpson**
Illustrated by **Fraser Williamson**

# Fast phonics

**Before reading this book, ask the student to practise saying the sounds (phonemes) and reading the new words used in the book. Try to make it as speedy and as fun as possible.**

## Read the tricky high frequency words

The student can't sound out these words at the moment, but they need to know them because they are commonly used.

go so

**Tip:** Encourage the student to sound out any sounds they know in these words, and you can provide them with the irregular or tricky part.

## Say the sounds

e k f

c h b d g o

**Tip:** Remember to say the pure sounds. For example, 'sssss' and 'nnnnn'. If you need a reminder, watch the *Snappy Sounds* videos.

## Snappy words

Point at a word randomly and have the student read the word. The student will need to sound out the word and blend the sounds to read the word. For example: 'K–i–m, Kim'.

ten fan set

fit Kat peg

Kim fog get

fig

## Quick vocabulary check

The underlined words may not be familiar to the student. Check their understanding before you start to read the book.

Kim and Kat met to get fit.

So fit!

Get set, Kim.
Get set, Kat. Go!

Can Kat get a peg?

Can Kim get a peg?

Kim got a bit hot.

Kat did not.

Kim got a peg.

Kat got ten!

So Kat got a pin
and a fig.

Kim got a fan!

Kim and Kat had a nap.

# Comprehension questions

## Let's talk about the story together

Ask the student:

- How did Kat and Kim get fit?
- How many pegs did Kat get?
- What is a fig?
- Why do you think Kim got hot?

## Snappy words

Ask the student to read these words as quickly as they can.

| set | get | peg | fit |
|---|---|---|---|
| fig | fog | fan | ten |

## Fluency

Can the student read the story again and improve on the last time?

Have fun!